THE SPIRIT OF THE SOUTH TOWARDS NORTHERN FREEMEN AND SOLDIERS DEFENDING THE AMERICAN FLAG AGAINST TRAITORS OF THE DEEPEST DYE.

BOSTON:
PUBLISHED BY R. F. WALLCUT,
No. 221 WASHINGTON STREET.
1861.

THE SPIRIT OF THE SOUTH.

Southern Humanity and Refinement. The following is one specimen only of a class of letters which are almost daily received by Gov. Andrew, of Massachusetts, from "*chivalrous*" gentlemen (?) in the Southern States:—

"Union Springs, Alabama,
Confederate States, May 6, 1861.

"Gov. Andrew:

"Sir,—We see in a New York paper that you have requested the authorities of Baltimore to send the bodies of the soldiers of your regiment that were killed at Baltimore back to Boston packed in ice, at the expense of the Commonwealth. We also see that you anticipate sending 200,000 men to coerce the South, to march from Washington City to Pensacola. Now, as it is very probable that some of these soldiers will be killed, we propose to take a contract for sending back their dead bodies, so as to be much cheaper to your people and give general satisfaction to their kindred. The following is our proposition:—

"For	the first thousand,	$50.00	per head.
"	ten "	37.50	"
"	thirty "	25.00	"
"	one hundred "	15.00	"

"We pledge ourselves to have them packed as quickly as possible after they are shot, so that the corpse will retain as much of his native bloom as possible.

"In all instances, commissioned officers will be charged double the above rates.

"Should your Excellency be pleased to give us the contract, we will thank you to notify us immediately, or as soon as the

Northern army crosses Mason and Dixon's line, for it will be necessary for whoever takes the contract to begin at that point, as Lee and Beauregard and Ben McCulloch and Jefferson Davis will be there to receive them, and will be very apt to *kill a few*—and we would regard it a great calamity for the Northern soldier to *spoil;* besides, we Southerners, in our *hot* climate, dislike offensive smells. After due reflection, and some *little Christian* consideration, we will be pleased to hear from you.

"Very respectfully, TONEY & WAUGH."

Ravings of a Virginia Editor. The Richmond (Va.) *Examiner* indulges in this highly amusing view of the North and its soldiers:—

"The North has no officers to command or drill the cowardly, motley crew of starving foreigners and operatives that it proposes to send South to fill ditches and as food for cannon, because it has no room in its penitentiaries and poor houses to receive or sustain them. The regular troops of the Union, since the resignation of the Southerners, are deficient in officers; and who are to drill and command the 75,000 militia sheep?

"If we except Benedict Arnold, there never was a Northern man who was fitted to command, if you would give him a chance to run. Like cowardly boys, when pent up on shipboard without a chance of escape, they gather courage from despair, and fight desperately. But with ninety-nine Northern men in a hundred, on all occasions, duty, honor, patriotism, has ever been considered a mere matter of profit and loss. Since the days of Washington, they have ever deemed that course of conduct by which most money is made and least risk incurred, the most virtuous and honorable.

"They will not come to Washington, they cannot be handcuffed and driven to Washington, if we only precede them, and let them see that they will have to fight for glory, and not for spoils and plunder. They never did fight, and never will fight, except for pay, for pillage and plunder. Once satisfy them that no money is to be made, no plunder to be gotten by invading the South, and no power on earth can lash and kick them south of Mason and Dixon's line."

"WEEPING WARRIORS." Under this caption, the New Orleans *Bulletin* indulges in the following effusion: —

"If we can credit the Northern journals, there must be in old Abe's officers very little of that sterner stuff soldiers are supposed to possess. Whenever or wherever they make their appearance, it is, like Niobe, all in tears. They weep when they surrender; weep when reinforced at some invested post; weep when ordered into service; weep for not being ordered into service, and weep even when the recipients of a great popular ovation. By the Rood, these Northern Paladins are o'er given to the melting mood. From the Lieutenant-General down to Lieut. Jones, who, in one night, ran all the way from Harper's Ferry to Carlisle Barracks, Pa., there rains such a flood of tears,

"That were the world on fire,
They might have drowned the wrath of Heaven,
And quenched the mighty ruin."

"But the latest and most affecting of all these exhibitions is the following, from the Providence *Journal*: —

"'We learn that when the Massachusetts troops arrived at Fort Munroe, the commander of the fort was moved to tears. He exclaimed, seizing the hand of their Colonel, "in Heaven's name, where did you get such noble-looking fellows as these?" He shook every man by the hand.'

"Well, if the greasy operatives of Lowell and Lawrence, and the smutty shoemakers of Lynn, be 'noble-looking fellows,' then language has lost its meaning. Probably the weeping commander, being a kind-hearted man, used the language attributed to him in the sense that Wordsworth somewhere says "the *meanest* things can call up thoughts that do often lie too deep for tears."

"Let patriotic citizens, then, go forth upon the trackless war paths of the ocean to fight for their country in the most effective manner. Hundreds and hundreds of millions of the property of the enemy invite them to spoil him — to 'spoil these Egyptians' of the North, who would coerce us to staying when we strove peaceably to make our exodus to independence of their oppressive thrall; to go forth from degrading fellowship with them. The richly laden ships of the enemy swarm on every sea, and are absolutely unprotected. The harvest is ripe; let it be gathered, and we will strike the enemy to the heart—for we hit his pocket, his most sensitive part. His treasure ships, laden with California wealth, traverse Southern waters. Let them be the prize of the bravest and most enterprising.

"His commerce is the very life of the enemy's solvency and financial vitality. Strike it, and you lay the axe to the root of his power—you rend away the sinews of war. Let the flags of privateers show themselves on the seas, and the blockade will be raised. Lincoln's fleet will scatter over the world to protect the commerce of his citizens. But they cannot protect it, though they try. They are numerous enough for the blockade, *but not to guard the ocean.* The risk of the privateer will still be trifling, *and he will continue to reap the harvest*, laughing at the few scarecrows which would fright him from his profitable employment.

"It is easy to put privateers afloat. There are an abundance of brave men among us ready to volunteer to fight any where. There are many among us ready to give money to the cause of their country, not looking for return. In this privateering, the most enormous returns are promised, with but trifling risk. Let the men of means fit out privateers if they would best serve their country and advance their own interests. Let companies be formed to embark capital in privateering. If they can't get the craft here, they can get them somewhere. It is a pursuit of honor, patriotism, profit. *Let us scour the sea, and sweep their commerce from it with the besom of destruction.*"—*Montgomery Advertiser.*

"We predict that Jeff. Davis will be on the banks of the Hudson within thirty days; that Mr. Lincoln will fly, with what little may be scraped together from a bankrupt Treasury, from Washington, and that Gen. Scott will bear him company; that nothing will be left a month hence of the Old Union, except possibly New England; and that the special session of Congress, called for the Fourth of July, will not meet nearer Washington than Portland, Maine, if it ever ets at all."—*Memphis Avalanche.*

"The proceedings of the brutal mobs in Philadelphia, New York, &c., are, of course, what might be expected of those sewers into which the whole world has poured its superfluous filth and scum. The action of these church-burning, flour-plundering, swinish groundlings, has no terrors for any but their Northern masters, the cowardly conservatives, or conservative cowards, who succumbed at the first onset of their white slaves. It is not only easy, but delightful, for bestial and craven natures to be ferocious and blood-thirsty where there is no danger, and Philadelphia, New York, &c., being supposed to be perfectly secure from bombardment, of course the dogs, wolves, hyenas, &c., had it all their own way.

"But upon the barbarians who compose the lower orders of the Northern cities, and who are much inferior in humanity and refinement to African negroes, it is a waste of ammunition to exhaust a single invective. The grossness and bestialities of these 'lewd fellows of the baser sort' are all upon the surface, and, therefore, bad as they are, they are not as contemptible as their masters. With some exceptions, the wealthy classes of the Northern cities are reptiles who have emerged from the same Stygian mud in which the more demonstrative and unclean mob are now wallowing, and in no wise differ from them except in their wealth, which has no power to confer elevated sentiments or purity of character.

"Consequently, as their own newspapers testify, the classes of those cities called conservative, which is but another name for men of money, are the most depraved and ignorant of any society in the world which pretends to social elevation and influence. It is believed that Paris, in its worst days, never equalled the corruptions of society among the fashionable classes in the Northern cities.

"For true conservatism, we have the most profound respect; and Heaven forbid that, in forming a new government, the South should have root or branch of the accursed levelling and agrarian spirit which has brought this country to its present ruin. But for the whited political and moral sepulchres of the North, called conservatives, simply because they have money in their purses, and seek to conserve it at the cost of a nation's peace and happiness, we have no sentiments but those of profound loathing and abhorrence."—*Richmond* (*Va.*) *Dispatch.*

"That the brutal fanatics who sit in the high places at Washington are ready to plunge the whole country into contest and blood, we have never doubted. It was a thorough conviction of their treacherous and desperate hatred of the South that compelled us to urge, as the only course of safety for the South, a prompt and eternal separation from their power.

"Events have shown that our estimation of this brutal and bloody faction was correct. Large portions of the people of the seceding States did not believe it. The frontier slave States have not believed it. They have still believed that there were feelings of respect, feelings of fraternity toward the people of the South, from the great body of the people of the North. Hence they have lingered in the foul embraces of a Union mastered by Abolitionism, whose one great policy was the subjugation of the South to the dominion of the North—whose one great passion was to destroy the South. Slowly, but surely, time has lifted the veil from the hideous and loathsome features of Abolitionism enthroned in Washington. Its inauguration by cannon and bayonets manifested at once its principle and its reliance for success—despotism and force. Oliver Cromwell, praying whilst Charles the First's head was being cut off, was the example of its bloody hypocrisy.

"With Lincoln's proclamation, and his requisition for troops to march upon the South, the standard for the conquest of the South is at last unfurled. Thirty years' agitation and hate at last breaks forth in its eager cries for blood. It is most natural. Thank God, the consummation is in our day, whilst yet we have the power to resist—the capacity to save ourselves from its meditated devastation, insurrection and horrors.

"But will Northern hate and fanaticism fail in its prey? Will it not at least carry through the South one long track of blood, which will tell to future ages its fierce invasion, and stern efforts for conquest? We answer, no!

"Fortunately for the world, it is never all mad. The first great result of the meditated invasion of the South will be to unite the South together. United together, the South is invincible. The North knows this as well as the South. On this account, we rejoice at the late demonstrations in Charleston Bay, and the war policy declared at Washington.

Virginia will soon be with us; and the other frontier States will follow her lead. They are forced to take sides by the Abolition government at Washington. They must help to conquer us, or aid us in our defence. We cannot doubt the result. The miserable fanatics and charletans at Washington are pursuing the very course of policy we most earnestly desire them to pursue, and will defeat and destroy their power for evil in their effort to exercise it. We deprecate war; but we frankly confess, that if war is necessary to consolidate the South, it is far preferable to the slaveholding States being divided. It is very far preferable to a mixed confederacy of slave and free States. The demonstration of war upon the South will, however, prevent war, by raising up such a power to meet it, through a united South, as will ensure its defeat."—*Charleston Mercury.*

A MODEL LETTER FROM A BALTIMORE SECESSIONIST. One of the valiant secessionists of Baltimore has written the following curious letter to his brother, a Union man:—

"BALTIMORE, Md., April 25, 1861.

"MY DEAR BROTHER,—I received your letter yesterday. All glad to hear from you. We have had stirring times in Baltimore since last Friday. We have driven back the hordes of negro worshippers from the North. It is really laughable to read the extracts from the New York papers about sacking and burning our city, when we have fed the half-starved slaves of Lincoln. On last Monday, we sent three car-loads of bread to the Pennsylvania paupers sent to attack us, and Baltimore told Lincoln to order them home, and he obeyed her. You have no idea of the war spirit here. Man and boy are all ready for the attempt to destroy us. In twelve hours, we could have sixty thousand men under arms, all eager for the fray. New York is a ruined city; the South is done with her for ever; her attitude towards her will not be forgotten soon. Maryland is out of the hateful Union—this will be the battle-ground. I beseech you not to volunteer against your native State. Your brothers and nephews will be in the ranks of old Maryland. I am so much excited, that I cannot write any more. *I am a rebel.*

"Your affectionate brother, * * *."

"The rapid enlistment at the North of 'Dead Rabbits, 'Plug Uglies,' 'Blood Tubs,' 'Jakies,' 'Soap Locks,' 'Bar-room Loungers,' 'Loafers,' 'Wharf-Rats,' 'Thieves,' and 'Pickpockets,' reminds us that it is time we had begun to organize, and prepare to defend our wives, our sisters, and our little ones from the menaces of a lawless horde that is now preparing for a descent upon our sacred hearthstones. Thousands of vagabonds at the North, with nothing else to do, are enlisting, not only for their bread, but the plunder that they expect to place their lawless grip upon. Men who have nothing to lose make the best thieves, and the outlawed scoundrels who are now filling the ranks of the Black Republican army are men who have no interest in common with humanity. Their nature is to prey upon their species, and they are prepared, like all other freebooters, to cut the throats of their neighbors, their fathers, or their brothers, for the sake of gold!

"To call them Judases would be a compliment, for that fallen disciple must have been possessed of the devil, and was prompted to betray and deliver the body of Christ, more by the influence of his Satanic Majesty than for the sake of the filthy lucre. But these mercenary hirelings, these Arnolds, are influenced alone by the thirty pieces of silver, and are not possessed of a sentiment half so sublime as that which the devil placed in the bosom of Judas.

"Is it to be supposed, then, that the Cut-Throats and Assassins, who sell themselves to the Typhon at Babylonish Washington, for Gold, for Booty, and for Beauty, will spare our homes and our household goods? Let no man lay that 'flattering unction to his soul,' but rather let us prepare for their defence, and wall them in with bristling bayonets, determined hearts and willing hands."—*Norfolk Day-Book.*

"The people of the North are either scared half out of their senses, or they are endeavoring to frighten us with their war bluster. By all accounts, they are raking their country from one extreme to the other, to catch every poor vagabond that they can either coax, buy or force to enlist."—*Savannah News.*

"We are ready for action—they are getting ready to prepare to act. They may raise plenty of men—men who prefer enlisting to starvation, scurvy fellows from the back slums of cities, whom Falstaff would not have marched through Coventry with; but these recruits are not soldiers, least of all, the soldiers to meet the hot-blooded, thorough-bred, impetuous men of the South. Trencher soldiers, who enlisted to war on their rations, not on men, they are—such as marched through Baltimore—squalid, wretched, ragged and half-naked, as the newspapers of that city report them. Fellows who do not know the breech of a musket from its muzzle, and had rather filch a handkerchief than fight an enemy in manly combat. White slaves, peddling wretches, small-change knaves and vagrants, the dregs and off-scourings of the populace—these are the levied 'forces' whom Lincoln suddenly arrays as candidates for the honor of being slaughtered by gentlemen such as Mobile sent to battle yesterday. Let them come South, and we will put our negroes to the dirty work of killing them. But they will not come South. Not a wretch of them will live on this side of the border longer than it will take us to reach the ground, and drive them over.

"Mobile is sending forth to wage this war of independence, the noblest and bravest of her sons. It is expensive, extravagant, to put such material against the riff-raff of mercenaries whom the abolition power has called out to war upon us. We could almost hope that a better class of men would fall into the Northern ranks, that our gentlemen might find foemen worthy of their steel, whom it would be more difficult to conquer, and whose conquering would be more honorable. For the present, however, we need not expect to find any foe worth fighting, with the exception of a few regiments, for the North is now getting ready, and will likely be whipped before it is ready."—*Mobile Evening News.*

"It is said that affairs in New York are in a very gloomy state, and that the people have no hopes of a better future state. Of course they haven't—Heaven was not intended for Black Republicans."—*New Orleans Delta.*

A writer in DeBow's *Review*, the ablest of the Southern magazines, gets quite beside himself in talking of the North. Hear him!

"Our Southern women are all conservatives, moral, religious, and sensitively modest, and abhor the North for infidelity, gross immorality, licentiousness, anarchy and agrarianism. 'T is they and the clergy who lead and direct the disunion movement. It is a gross mistake to suppose that abolition alone is the cause of dissension between the North and South. The Cavaliers, Jacobites and Huguenots, who settled the South, naturally hate, condemn and despise the Puritans, who settled the North. The former are master races—the latter a slave race, the descendants of the Saxon serfs. The former are Mediterranean races, descendants of the Romans; for Cavaliers and Jacobites are of Norman descent, and so were the Huguenots. The Saxons and Anglos, the ancestors of the Yankees, came from the cool and marshy regions of the North, where man is little more than a cold-blooded, amphibious biped.

"We are the most aristocratic people in the world. Pride of caste and color and privilege makes every man an aristocrat in feeling. Aristocracy is the only safeguard of liberty, the only power watchful and strong enough to exclude monarchical despotism. At the North, the progress and tendency of opinion is to pure democracy, less government, anarchy and agrarianism. Their hatred of the South will accelerate this noxious current of opinion, and anarchy will soon wind up in military despotism. There will be as many little despots as there are now States, for no usurper will wield means sufficient to conquer or fuse into one several States. It will be a great improvement in Northern affairs, and is far preferable to Northern Democracy, agrarianism, infidelity and free love."

"Virginia is the particular object of abolition envy, hatred and arrogance. As the doomed and damned of Tophet hate the blessed in Paradise, so do the mean, hungry, avaricious, lying, cheating, hypocritical, cunning, cowardly Yankees hate the high-toned, elevated Southerner, but, above all, the Virg nian."—*Richmond Examiner.*

MEN IN BUCKRAM. The New Orleans *True Delta* says:

"It is really refreshing this ardent weather to read the lucubrations of the Northern journals, each one of them, from the infamous *Herald* to the slimy *Journal of Commerce*, trying to outdo its mendacious neighbor in lying upon the most stupendous and patriotic scale. The immense armies these individuals proclaim as springing like Macgregor's clansmen from every bunch of heather, eager to devour these States, niggers and all, are, in our opinion, in buckram only; mighty upon muster rolls, but few and far between upon marching occasions. That a good many can be got to go to Washington, we do not doubt; pastures thereabout are pleasant, and when open gratis to all visitors, agreeable and welcome; but when it comes to the turn of Patterson, or Butler, or Cushing, honest Caleb, to try their 'prentice hands at war making to the South of the Potomac, our belief is that they will be missing.

"Virginia, we think, can hold her own against all the armies this description of men will lead against her, without any other aid than her own fighting resources will furnish; still, as her climate is inviting, and her hospitality of world-wide recognition, we would wish our gallant young soldiers now sickening upon the Metaire ridge an early safe deliverance from that locality and its execrable commissariat, and to get the route for Richmond. When there, if Butler and Cushing should find followers from the Massachusetts men, or the terrible New York Seventh, other than such deserters, the country will be delighted, and for once in their lives these worthies will have a chance of meeting that retribution which sooner or later never fails to reach the betrayer of principle, the enemy of right, the venal conspirator, and the traitor, in all of which characters they have appeared and flourished. Let the Abolition and Breckinridge Democratic journals of the North continue to call for the destruction of the South; it inspires no more uneasiness than the incoherent gibberish of the drivelling idiot, for they well know it means nothing, and that those who most vociferously unite in making the cry will be the very last to undertake the experiment of putting it into execution. The people are bewildered, but their enemies tremble in the presence of the spirit they have raised."

The New Orleans *Delta*—the organ of the buccaneering horde which makes that city its head quarters—thus speaks of the enlightened masses of the free States. The last we heard from the *Delta*, (says the Boston *Transcript*,) its agent was in Boston soliciting subscribers, on the ground that it was a Union paper. He obtained about a hundred names, at ten dollars each. That paper now says:—

"There is no doubt that the Northern people are at this moment fit representatives of the barbarian hordes which formerly devastated the world. They are furnishing the very best evidence that they are incapable of thorough civilization; that they possess only the outward symbols of modern enlightenment, while they are by nature cruel, blood-thirsty, arrogant and boastful. But there is really very little danger to be feared from them. Civilization no longer stands in dread of barbarism. One race of savages has already been expelled from the country; but not that it may fall into the hands of another. The Northern people may exhibit all the ferocity of the Huns, but they will never find an Attila to lead them to the conquest of the South."

The following article, copied from the Richmond *Examiner*, is a choice specimen of the appeals put forth to concentrate a rebel force on Washington:—

"The capture of Washington city is perfectly within the power of Virginia and Maryland, if Virginia will only make the proper effort by her constituted authorities; nor is there a single moment to lose. The entire population pant for the onset; there never was half the unanimity amongst the people before, not a tithe of the zeal, upon any subject, that is now manifested to take Washington, and drive from it every Black Republican who is a dweller there. From the mountain tops and valleys to the shores of the sea, there is one wild shout of fierce resolve to capture Washington at all and every human hazard. The filthy cage of unclean birds must and will assuredly be purified by fire. The people are determined upon it,. and are clamorous for a leader to conduct them to the onslaught. That leader will assuredly arise, aye, and that right speedily.

"It is not to be endured that this flight of Abolition harpies shall come down from the black North for their roosts in the heart of the South, to defile and brutalize the land. They come as our enemies—they act as our most deadly foes—they promise us bloodshed and fire, and this is the only promise they have ever redeemed. The fanatical yell for the immediate subjugation of the whole South is going up hourly from the united voices of all the North; and for the purpose of making their work sure, they have determined to hold Washington city as the point from whence to carry on their brutal warfare.

"Our people can take it—they will take it—and Scott, the arch traitor, and Lincoln, the beast, combined, cannot prevent it. The just indignation of an outraged and deeply injured people will teach the Illinois Ape to repent his course, and retrace his journey across the borders of the free negro States still more rapidly than he came; and Scott, the traitor, will be given an opportunity at the same time to try the difference between 'Scott's tactics' and the Shanghai drill for quick movements.

"Great cleansing and purification are needed, and will be given to the festering sink of iniquity, that wallow of Lincoln and Scott—the desecrated city of Washington—and many indeed will be the carcasses of dogs and catiffs that will blacken the air upon the gallows, before the great work is accomplished. So let it be."

"It seems that Washington City is the destination of most of Lincoln's levies. He is evidently determined to secure the protection of his own person against the approaches of the 'secessionists,' who doubtless haunt his midnight dreams. He could not play his card more effectually in the interests of the South. When he collects as many of his trainbands around him as he may deem essential to his safety, the armies of the South will close in upon them, as the hunter draws his net upon the luckless covey that find their way into its folds in the blindness of ignorance and fear. Maryland and Virginia have joined the South in time to participate in this rare sport."—*Jackson Mississippian.*

"A squad of Massachusetts militia, confronted by an equal number of Mississippi riflemen, would make better time than ever Lexington made over the Metaire course. Massachusetts pluck and prowess are terrible on paper, but on paper only. The down-easters of Massachusetts are now avowing their ability and their intention of whipping the Southerners, to use their own classic language, 'to all darnation.' When it comes to the pinch, they will simmer down more quickly than the well-known individual, whose call for the man that struck Billy Patterson was so promptly and unexpectedly answered. The South, so it is threatened, is to be invaded by an army of codfish and onion-fed warriors from the State of Maine. At the first fire from Bragg's or Beauregard's battery, they will scatter like a parcel of young chickens when they see the hungry hawk swooping down on them from the upper air."—*New Orleans Crescent.*

"The cowardly 'eighteen millions' North told us we should not leave the Union. We did it openly and boldly, and they humbly acknowledge our government 'as a necessity.' They shouted the praises of the 'stars and stripes,' and dared the 'chivalry' 'to touch the sacred emblem.' We have torn it down; we have placed in its stead the flag of the Confederate States; we have dared them to 'coerce' us and resent the insult; we have invited their vaunted numbers to the field; but the only cry that comes from the craven dogs is, 'military necessity'; 'give up the forts'; 'withdraw the troops'; let us 'eat dirt and live.' It is sickening to think of ever having lived in the same government with such a people; but let us rejoice at our separation, and look southward. The game North is beneath contempt, while Mexico invites us, by invasion of Texas, to reënact our former achievements."—*Houston (Texas) Patriot.*

WANTED—5000 Washerwomen, with broomsticks, to whip back Governor Sprague's regiment from Rhode Island, lately offered to Lincoln.

CODFISH & INGUNS.

—*Augusta (Ga.) paper.*

MORE SOUTHERN "HONOR." The following is a copy of a letter received by Mr. Lyman Dike, a shoe dealer in Boston. It needs no comment: such specimens of Southern honor and honesty have become too common to excite much remark:—

"COLUMBIA, S. C., May, 1861.

"LYMAN DIKE, ESQ.,—I have collected three hundred dollars and twenty-three cents for you, and also for O. M. Hitchings three hundred and seventy-eight dollars and twenty-six cents, the notes for which said amounts were given; you have my receipt for collection. The above amounts are deposited in the Branch of the Bank of the State of South Carolina at Columbia. I noticed, some time ago, that the citizens of Boston were paying twenty dollars per month for hirelings to invade and subjugate the South. I will retain the above sums in my hands to assist in the payment for powder and ball expended upon your city hirelings, and the balance will be applied to give them a more decent burial than they would probably get at home.

"Yours, &c., J. H. PIERSON."

The Mobile *Register* of May 1st cheats itself and its readers with the following delectable romances:—

"The Massachusetts troops which were so roughly handled by the people of Baltimore were half armed, badly clothed, and nearly starved. Their colonel behaved like a dastard, gave his men the order to 'run,' and sheltered himself under the wing of the Mayor.

"At Gosport, where by Lincoln's order the public property was burned, all the accounts show that the naval and military officers and men to whom that vandal work was entrusted, behaved in a most cowardly manner, and all hands were drunk, from Commodore Macaulay down.

"The five thousand rowdies who seized Cairo are represented as the scourings of the city of Chicago and other Western towns, and they amuse themselves with stopping unarmed boats and stealing hen-coops. An eye-witness says that one thousand firm Southern men could run them from the town, unless the mosquitoes and chills and fever save them the trouble in the meantime. Throughout the war, so far, not one act of courage, not one symptom of generalship and soldierly feeling or ability, have been displayed. Lincoln himself is frightened to death, keeps up his spirits by pouring spirits down, sleeps with his boots on, and his 'cap and cloak' at hand, with his palace filled with armed men to guard his sacred person. The Government, and the military and the press in its service, are exhibiting at every step unmistakable signs of trepidation.

"Woe be to the Northern battalions that meet the first shock and outburst of the fiery valor and fierce indignation that have fused in one compact mass the entire Southern mind and heart! If the war lasts five years, the terms of peace will be dictated at the gates of Boston. But the war will not last so long. The day is not far distant when the North will sue for peace. Until it does, the policy as well as the will of the South is to give them war to their hearts' content—war to the knife and to the hilt."

"Gypsies and free negroes have many amiable, noble, and generous traits; Yankees, sourkrout Germans and Canadians none. Senator Wade says, and Seward, too, that the North will absorb Canada. They are half true; the vile, sensual, animal, brutal, infidel, superstitious democracy of Canada and the Yankee States will coalesce; and Senator Johnson, of Tennessee, will join them. But when Canada and Western New York, and New England, and the whole beastly, puritanic, 'sourkrout,' free negro, infidel, superstitious, licentious, democratic population of the North become the masters of New York—what then? Outside of the city, the State of New York is Yankee and Puritanical; composed of as base, unprincipled, superstitious, licentious, and agrarian and anarchical population as any on earth. Nay, we do not hesstate to say that it is the vilest population on earth. If the city does not secede and erect a separate republic, this population, aided by the ignorant, base, brutal, sensual German infidels of the Northwest, the stupid democracy of Canada, (for Canada will in some way coalesce with the North,) and the arrogant and tyrannical people of New England, will become masters of the destinies of New York."—*De Bow's Review.*

The sort of stuff which passes for news in the Southern States seems to be growing more and more absurd. For instance, in the Charleston *Courier*, of April 29, we find these items:—

"We learn from a passenger from Philadelphia, that one day last week, at Havre-de-Grace, three of the Northern volunteers who were marched from the North refused to go any further, assigning as a reason that they did not volunteer to go into a war of invasion upon the South. An officer who was standing by instantly cut and hacked two of the men to pieces. A third, who took the same ground, gave vent to a similar expression for the Union, cut his own throat from ear to ear, rather than allow himself to be hacked to pieces.

"Mob law [in New York city] is triumphant, and Southern men, or those known to sympathize with the South, are in constant danger of their lives. Vigilance committees visit the houses of the wealthy, and every man is heavily assessed for the support of the families of those who have volunteered their services to the Administration. Assessments of $5,000, $3,000 and $2,000 on large houses are said to be very common. Those merchants who refuse, or make the slightest hesitation, are threatened with the cleaning out of their stores, and several already have been emptied by the mob.

"Three men were set upon in Florence Hotel, New York, and two killed, for expressing sympathy with the South.

"Merchants are packing off their clerks, and it is said that several large manufactories have been stopped with a view of forcing the operatives into the ranks of the volunteer soldiery."

The Raleigh (N. C.) *Banner*, urging an attack upon Washington, says:—

"The army of the South will be composed of the best material that ever yet made up an army; whilst that of Lincoln will be gathered from the sewers of the cities—the degraded, beastly offscourings of all quarters of the world will serve for pay, and run away just as soon as they can, when danger threatens them."

The following insulting letter has been sent to the President, who is in frequent receipt of such malignant effusions:

"DEMOPOLIS, Alabama,
Confederate States of America, April, 1861.

"HIS EXCELLENCY, ABRAHAM LINCOLN:

"Sir,—I have just read your proclamation calling for 75,000 mercenaries to invade these States. With all proper respect, I offer you a wager of $50,000, that we meet you half way, and whip you and your Yankee hosts.

"Respectfully, ALFRED HATCH.

"P. S. If the bet is accepted, the money will be deposited in the Farmers' Bank of Virginia."

A POLITE INVITATION. Troops from the South and Southwest continue to pour into Virginia. They all go armed and equipped, and when Abraham orders his mercenaries to invade Old Virginia, they will be met by not less than 100,000 well drilled and thoroughly disciplined troops, and after the first battle, won't the vultures have a good time feeding on Yankee carcasses? Come on, *Abraham*, you are wanted! Old Scott, we hope, will head the invading force. If so, his bones will be apt to rot on the soil which he has disgraced by his treachery.—*Newbern Progress.*

THE POISONING POLICY. A letter from Pensacola to a Mobile paper gives an account of an interview between a U. S. officer on board of the Powhatan, and a Capt. Thompson, whose craft had been overhauled, wherein the officer expressed a desire to purchase fresh butter, eggs, vegetables, &c. The writer adds—

"Here 's a chance now to play old Greeley's game—strychnine the last rascal of an officer; rat soup the marines, and drench the sailors with chain-lightning whisky. Any thing, any thing to get rid of these hateful ships and their crews."

A correspondent of the Charleston *Courier*, writing from Richmond, anticipates an attack upon that city, "the gem of the State, the Koh-i-noor upon which Lincoln and that twin-hearted brother of his, the recreant Scott, are feasting their gaze as the richest prize of the South." "Possibly," he says, "the 'glorious Seventh,' that orchestra of military virtues, will lead the vanguard—'glorious' in their clean faces, languishing side whiskers, good clothes, white kids and patent leather boots; and possibly they may be received, but not as before. It will be a 'welcome with bloody hands to hospitable graves.' Zouaves, rowdies, New York thieves and cut-throats, mingled with a hodge-podge of Jerseymen, Rhode Islanders, Massachusetts men, wooden-nutmeg Yankees and Down-Easters, may also come—a solid, gaping phalanx; but they will be met by a wall of Southern hearts, who will turn them in their tracks, or annihilate them from their soil. There is a great difference between fighting for wages or for an abstract idea, and fighting for mothers, wives and sisters. 'Beauty and booty' may be a tempting motto with which to invade your neighbor's fireside, but it is one which wipes out all the landmarks of civilized warfare, and will secure for its follower the fate of the brute."

The Memphis *Avalanche* says:—"It is painful to see the Chair at Washington disgraced by such a degraded, drunken wretch as Abe Lincoln. Our reverence for the Father of his Country makes us anxious to see the city bearing his honored name rid of such a caricature of a President." The same print persistently accuses "old Abe"—as honest an old tee-totaller as ever lived—of habitual drunkenness, and says the President became addicted to this vice in this way:—"The cares of place affected his nervous system so much that he could not sleep. His physician administered to him large quantities of opium and brandy each evening until stupidity would ensue, and then he would fall into profound slumber. In the morning, his prostration would become so great that liquor would be resorted to; and thus, by a frequent repetition of this treatment, he has become so demoralized by the use of liquors as to be perfectly imbecile, and thoroughly indifferent to what is passing around him."

"We have much to do. We shall be necessitated to whip them soundly—to burn a few of their towns—to capture Washington as a city, or enter it as a heap of ruins; we will have to cripple their commerce with privateers; burn their factories, and reduce them to the condition of begging peace, instead of graciously condescending to grant us a separate existence with peace, as we have besought. Every thing leads to this opinion. They are distracted among themselves. Their resources are crippled; their toiling millions are suffering already; their sober, thinking men acknowledge that madness rules their every movement, and none who view things as they are can for a moment believe that success will crown their efforts.

"On our part, we have hundreds of thousands of men well armed, ready to take the field at a moment's warning. We are united in every way, with the consciousness of a just cause, and, above all, with *millions* of dollars at our command."—*Montgomery corr. Charleston Courier.*

"The people of the Monumental City were right in arresting the progress of an army raised to shoot down their Southern brethren. We hope they will keep up the good work, and even strike at home for their honor and independence. There are slumbering fires, not only in Maryland but in States north of her, that await only an opportunity to burst forth, and when they appear, we may look out for a revolution that the world now little expects. Thank God! the time has arrived when these minions of Abolition can never plant a foot south of the Potomac. Virginia will see to it, if tried, that they repent the experiment."—*Savannah Republican.*

All to be Butchered. The leading papers of the Lincoln party at the North declare that the people of the South shall be butchered like dogs, and their property divided out among the soldiers who fight for Lincoln. They threaten our wives and our little ones with the most inhuman butchery, and talk of setting fire to our dwellings and wiping us from the very face of the earth.—*Milledgeville Federal Union.*

The Tallahassee *Sentinel* has just learned how Mr. Lincoln lives. It says:—

"Lincoln keeps five men in his room to guard him by night, and Mrs. Lincoln two to guard her. Old Abe, in order to keep his spirits and courage up, 'pours the spirits down,' and is half drunk all the time. For fear of being poisoned, Mrs. Lincoln has turned cook, and prepares all the food they eat. Some ministers of the Gospel recently called to see him, to entreat him to desist from his mad policy of coercion, when the indignant Abe cursed them away, swearing that the Southerners should wade knee-deep in blood before entering Washington city."

"But one course is left for all honorable Southern men to pursue: that is, to get ready for battle. The man that doubts is damned; he that dallies is a dastard. We feel no apprehension as to the patriotism of the people of the Confederate States. An army of seventy-five thousand men, backed by volunteers from the Border States, will soon be organized by President Davis. But we must not only be ready to defend our homes, our families and firesides: we must carry the war into Africa. We must attack the Black Republican citadel, and drive out its infamous garrison. Let Washington city be the point of attack, and an army of 100,000 men be marched against it."—*Federal Union, Milledgeville, Ga.*

The following is an extract of a letter from New Orleans, dated April 10:—

"I start in a few days at the head of a thousand of the best men you ever saw, with Maynard rifles and Colt's navy revolvers. We think we can whip five Abolitionists to one of us. We may meet some of you at Washington—if so, look out for the top of your heads at a thousand yards."

"We learn from a gentleman who saw this regiment [the Massachusetts 6th] at Baltimore, that it is composed of the meanest-looking, whiskey-swilling, rum-head ragamuffins that he had ever seen."—*Montgomery Mail.*

"Our citizens feel considerable relief at getting rid ot Gen. Butler—in other words, *Picayune* or *Strychnine* Butler—who was in command for some days of this military division. A more conceited or bigger fool has not appeared in Baltimore since the National Democratic Convention last spring, when the same popinjay coxcomb was here figuring as a great Breckinridge man. Our citizens of intelligence and polite attainments, who were obliged to come in official contact with him, were absolutely disgusted. Supreme respect for law and order alone prevented his getting into difficulty. Fancy the old mush-head seated upon a charger, armed with sword and pistols, a cigar in his mouth and half tight, surrounded by his staff and body guard, riding the streets in open day, blustering like a swelled frog, assuming importance much beyond what that reptile did when it swelled to bursting at beholding the ox. Thank fortune, 'Picayune Butler' has gone from town, as is well understood, at the bidding of his master, and left a gentleman—Gen. Cadwallader—to adorn the position he cumbered with a mountebank."—*Baltimore corr. Charleston Courier.*

The Charleston *Mercury*, after saying that the officers clothed with power by the voice of the people "would fly like rats out of a burning barn," out-Herods Herod thus:—

"Let them go. Do not pollute the soil of Virginia or Maryland with their mean blood. Let them go. To keep them in Washington, after Virginia and Maryland have seceded, you will have to put them in a three-story jail. Do not dignify them by chasing them—much less killing them."

"If one half the Northern people feel and think as we infer from their papers—and they represent a vast majority in every State—we would as soon confederate with the cannibals of the South Sea or the Thugs of India as with them. They have forced us to the separation, and now, we say, let it be for ever—and even beyond that time, should God in his providence permit. We want nothing to do with such a people, either in time or eternity."—*Savannah Republican.*

www.ingramcontent.com/pod-product-compliance
Lightning Source LLC
LaVergne TN
LVHW011145110826
845150LV00008B/2522

9781418192105